Do you see the little blue fish?

Do you see the little orange cat?

What Do You See?

by Heather Flaherty

SCHOLASTIC INC.

Photos ©: cover: Mitsuaki Iwago/Minden Pictures; 3: David Chapman/Alamy; 4: Michael Fogden/ Earth Scenes/Animals Animals; 5: Stocktrek Images, Inc./Alamy; 6: NaturePL/SuperStock; 7: Karen Ulvestad/Alamy; 8 Top Center: Dmitri Illarionov/Dreamstime; 8 Bottom Center: zigifoto/Getty Images; 8 top right: Michael Fogden/ Earth Scenes/Animals Animals; 8 bottom left: Stocktrek Images, Inc./Alamy; All other photos © Shutterstock.com.

Designed by Amy Lam.

Printed in the U.S.A.
Produced by Clean Slate Press Ltd.

ISBN-13: 978-0-545-66652-7
ISBN-10: 0-545-66652-X

13 14 15 16 17 18 19 20 165 29 28 27 26 25 24 23 22

Scholastic Inc., 557 Broadway, New York, NY 10012

Do you see the little brown dog?

Do you see the little yellow chick?

Do you see the little green frog?

Do you see the little white horse?

What do you see?

little brown dog

little yellow chick

little green frog

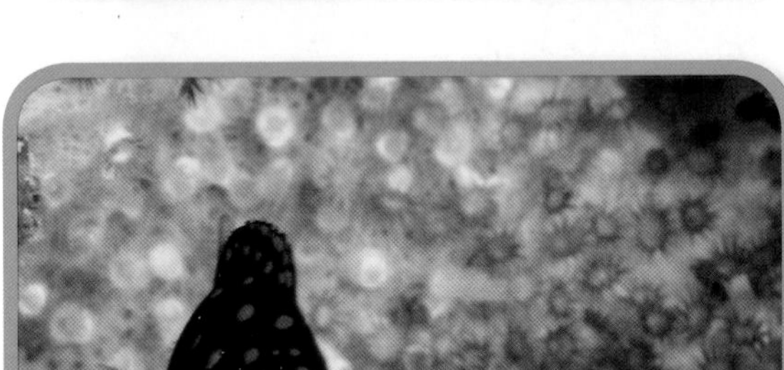
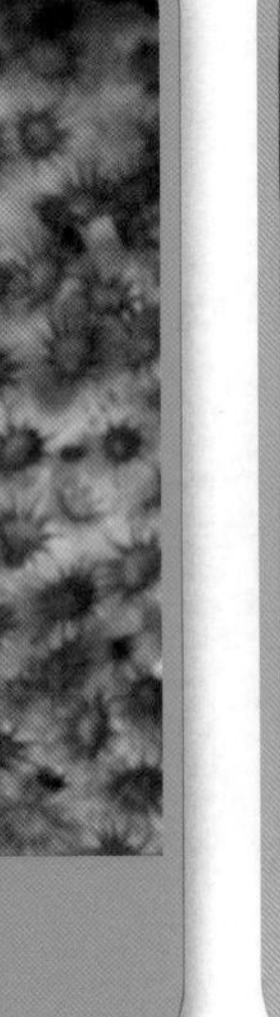

little blue fish

little orange cat

little white horse